Let's Have Fun Outside!

LET'S PLAY IN THE SNOW

By Kristen Rajczak Nelson

Gareth Stevens
PUBLISHING

Please visit our website, www.garethstevens.com. For a free color catalog of all our high-quality books, call toll free 1-800-542-2595 or fax 1-877-542-2596.

Library of Congress Cataloging-in-Publication Data

Names: Rajczak Nelson, Kristen, author.
Title: Let's play in the snow / Kristen Rajczak Nelson.
Description: Buffalo, New York : Gareth Stevens Publishing, [2025] |
   Series: Let's have fun outside! | Includes index.
Identifiers: LCCN 2023045715 | ISBN 9781482465891 (library binding) | ISBN
   9781482465884 (paperback) | ISBN 9781482465907 (ebook)
Subjects: LCSH: Snow–Juvenile literature. | Winter–Juvenile literature. |
   Outdoor recreation for children–Juvenile literature.
Classification: LCC QC926.37 .R33 2025 | DDC 551.57/84–dc23/eng/20231011
LC record available at https://lccn.loc.gov/2023045715

Published in 2025 by
Gareth Stevens Publishing
2544 Clinton Street
Buffalo, NY 14224

Designer: Claire Zimmermann
Editor: Kristen Nelson

Photo credits: Cover, p. 1 Odua Images/Shutterstock.com; p. 5 Gajus/Shutterstock.com; p. 7
Serhii Hrebeniuk/Shutterstock.com; pp. 9, 24 (middle) Yuliia Gornostaieva/Shutterstock.com;
p. 11 Ami Parikh/Shutterstock.com; p. 13 morrowlight/Shutterstock.com; p. 15 Evgeny
Atamanenko/Shutterstock.com; p. 17 Sergey Novikov/Shutterstock.com; p. 19 Jaren Jai Wicklund/
Shutterstock.com; pp. 21, 24 (right) Tatiana Buzmakova/Shutterstock.com; pp. 23, 24 (left)
MNStudio/Shutterstock.com.

CPSIA compliance information: Batch #CSGS25: For further information contact Gareth Stevens, at 1-800-542-2595.

Find us on

Contents

It is winter.
It is cold.
Look at the
snow outside!

Let's play in the snow!
We need to wear boots.
They keep our feet dry.

Olivia has a pink hat.
She puts on
pink mittens.

Jacen wears
snow pants.
He stays warm and dry!

Thea lays in the snow.
She makes a
snow angel!

Paulie and Devra roll
big balls of snow.
They make a snowman!
I add a carrot nose.

We make snowballs.
We throw them around!

My brother brings out
his sled.
We walk to the big hill.
We sled down!

Kristi takes a turn.
Her sled is yellow!

Time to warm up!
Dad gets us hot cocoa.

Words to Know

cocoa

mittens

sled

Index